Walkthrough

This is another story about Josie. What other books about Josie have we read?

Let's read the title together: 'Josie's New Coat'.

What sort of coat is Josie looking at?

Do you think she likes it?

Walkthrough

Let's read the blurb together.

What sort of coat do you think she will get?

Walkthrough

Let's read the title again: 'Josie's New Coat'.

Do you like this coat?

Is it the same as on the cover?

Walkthrough

Why have they gone into this shop?

The sign in the window says 'special offer'.

Observe and Prompt

Word Recognition

- Check the children can read the word 'coat' using their decoding skills. Help them with the 'oa' vowel sound if they have difficulty.
- If the children have difficulty reading 'new', help them with the 'ew' sound.
- Check the children apply their phonic knowledge when reading 'fluffy', blending from left to right through the word.

Josie and Mum went out.
They went to get a new coat
for Josie.

2

Walkthrough

What sort of coat does Josie want?

How can you tell?

"Can I have a red coat
or a fluffy coat?" said Josie.

3

Observe and Prompt

Language Comprehension

- Check the children recognise speech and read it with appropriate expression.
- Ask the children where Josie and Mum are going. What are they going to buy?
- What sort of coat do the children think Josie wants?
- What do the children think Josie will do next?

Walkthrough

What's Mum looking at?

What's Josie looking at?

Observe and Prompt

Word Recognition

- Check the children can read 'saw' using their decoding skills. Help them with the 'aw' sound if they have trouble.
- If the children have difficulty reading the word 'looked', help them with the 'ed' suffix at the end of this word.
- Check the children can read the sight word 'some'.

Josie and Mum went to look
at the coats.
Mum looked at some red coats.
Josie looked at some fluffy coats.

4

Walkthrough

What sort of coat has Josie chosen?

Josie saw a fluffy coat.

5

Observe and Prompt

Language Comprehension

- Ask the children which coats Josie looks at.
- Which coat do the children think Josie likes best?
- Do the children think Josie will try the coats on?

Walkthrough

Do Mum and Josie like the fluffy coat?

What is the problem with the fluffy coat?

Observe and Prompt

Word Recognition

- Check the children can read the word 'all'. If they have difficulty, model the reading of this word for them.
- Check the children can read the CVC words 'Mum', 'big' and 'red' using their decoding skills.
- Check the children are reading 'coats' and 'coat' with more confidence.

"I like it!" said Josie.
"I like it too," said Mum,
"but it's too big.
All the fluffy coats are too big."

6

Walkthrough

Which coat has Josie chosen now?

Josie saw a red coat.

7

Observe and Prompt

Language Comprehension

- Ask the children which coat Josie and Mum like.
- Ask the children what the problem is with the fluffy coat.
- Do the children think Josie will try on the red coat? Will it fit?

Walkthrough

What's wrong with the red coat?

Will any of the red coats fit?

Observe and Prompt

Word Recognition

- Check the children can read 'little' using their decoding skills. Help them with the 'le' sound if they have difficulty.
- Check the children can read the word 'too'.
- If the children have difficulty with 'can't', model the blending of this word for them.

Walkthrough

How do you think Josie feels?

Why is she disappointed?

"So I can't have a fluffy coat,"
said Josie.
"And I can't have a red coat."

9

Observe and Prompt

Language Comprehension

- Check the children are reading the speech with appropriate expression.
- Ask the children how they think Josie feels. Why?
- Which coat do the children think Josie will try on next?

Walkthrough

What do these coats look like?

Do you think Josie likes them?

Observe and Prompt

Word Recognition

- Check the children can read the words 'Then' and 'these' using their decoding skills.
- Check the children can read 'blue' using their decoding skills. Help them with the 'ue' sound if they struggle.
- Check the children can read 'yellow' using their decoding skills. If they have difficulty, help them with the 'ow' sound.

Then Mum saw some red and
blue and yellow coats.
"Look at these coats, Josie,"
said Mum.
Josie put on a coat.

10

Walkthrough

Does Mum like this coat?

How does Josie feel about the coat?

"I like it!" said Mum.
"Do you like it, Josie?"

11

Observe and Prompt

Language Comprehension

- Observe the children read the direct speech with phrasing and expression, taking note of punctuation.
- Ask the children which coat Josie tries on now.
- Do the children think she likes it? How can they tell?

Walkthrough

Does Josie like the coat?

Is she sure about that?

How do you know?

Observe and Prompt

Word Recognition

- Check the children can read the word 'Yes' using their decoding skills.
- If the children have difficulty with the word 'take', help them with the long 'a' sound (from 'a' and silent 'e').
- Check the children can read 'this' using their decoding skills.

Walkthrough

What is Mum doing now?

How can you tell Josie is not that happy?

Mum said, "We will take this coat."

13

Observe and Prompt

Language Comprehension

- Check the children are reading 'Y-Y-Y-Yes' with expression. Prompt them to look at the way it is written.
- How can the children tell that Josie is not happy with her new coat?
- What do the children think will happen next?

Walkthrough

Where is Josie going now?

What is she wearing?

Observe and Prompt

Word Recognition

- If the children have difficulty with the word 'school', model the reading of this word for them.
- If the children have difficulty reading 'Ravi' and 'Tilly', model the blending of these words for them.

Josie went to school
in her new coat.

14

Walkthrough

Who can Josie see on the bus?

Observe and Prompt

Language Comprehension

- Ask the children what Josie is wearing.
- Ask the children who Josie sees on the bus.
- How do the children think Josie feels? Why doesn't she want to see her friends?

Walkthrough

What are Ravi and Tilly wearing?

How are the three of them feeling?

Observe and Prompt

Word Recognition

- Check the children can read 'I've'. Model the reading of this word for them if they have difficulty.

Observe and Prompt

Language Comprehension

- Check for expressive reading and phrasing.
- Ask the children what has happened at the end.
- Ask the children why it is a funny ending.

THE ANDALUCIAN HORSE

Tim Blake

A Square One Publication

First published in 1991 by Square One Publications
Saga House, Sansome Place Worcester WR1 1UA

British Library Cataloguing in Publication Data
Blake, Tim G.
The Andalucian Horse
1. Horses
1. Title
636.13

ISBN 1-872017-35-5

Cover design by Tony de Saulles

Typeset by Wyvern Typesetting, Worcester
in Palacio 11 point on 14 point

Printed by Acanthus Press Ltd,
Wellington, Somerset, England.

To Judy, who combines the roles of
wife and best friend, and who arranged
all the photographic work in this book

My special thanks to Snr. Gonzalo Argüeso Piñar
of Seville for his advice and
practical help in the preparation
of the material for this book.

Contents

Foreword

Tim Blake's book opens the door to a fascinating world that is a blend of skill and expertise combined with colour and gaiety. This is the world of the Andalusian horse of Spain.

Each stage of the book makes the reader eager for more information on that particular section and so makes this book compulsive to read. At the end of each part of the book one is avidly waiting for a sequel, or next instalment.

The fact that it is written by someone who has genuinely fallen in love with a breed of horse that has led him to acquaint himself thoroughly with all its many aspects, makes the actual reading of the book a very enjoyable experience. In addition the plentiful and excellent photographs produced by Judy Blake enhance the book and take the reader more deeply into the Andalusian world.

My own appreciation of the breed occurred in 1972 when, to celebrate the 400th anniverary of the Spanish Riding School, Alverez Domecq accompanied by his son Alvaro, brought a team of Andalusians to Vienna and one was given the opportunity to meet some of the riders. Side by side with the Lippizanner, one could see many similar traits, and both breeds in my opinion have many endearing qualities, but from the Teutonic background the Lippizanner showed a more controlled discipline compared with the Latin background of the Andalusian. One could almost see the tempestuous clapping of castanets and stamping of heels in the Andalusian's bearing, with his long mane and tail and his accentuated elevated stride.

In his book Tim Blake leads us through history and dressage development right into the heart of Andalusia and Jerez. One cannot help but to mentally book a flight to this lesser known area of Spain and see for oneself the Domecq School, the Doma Vaquera competitions, the Studs and even the skill of the Rejoneador.

I am sure once there if the African horse sickness epidemic permits, one would be hard pressed not to return home with an Andalusian Horse.

John F. Lassetter B.H.S.I.
Goodwood April 1991

1
History

Few breeds have had as much influence on the modern horse as the Andalucian. Possibly, the Arabian comes close to this most ancient breed in supplying blood lines to the great modern breeds. Nevertheless, it is an irony that during this century the Andalucian has suffered a general decline in popularity and flourishes only in its own native land and in small pockets elsewhere. There are a number of flourishing Andalucian studs in America, and in the United Kingdom the British Andalucian Horse Society is doing its best to popularise the breed. In spite of these efforts, there is still a very real danger of the breed becoming of interest mainly to collectors of the unusual and suffering a fate similar to its close relative, the Lippizaner. The famous white horses of Vienna still attract good crowds to their performances which display a degree of baroque splendour but they are seldom encountered outside their rather gilded surroundings.

And yet the Andalucian is far more than just a "showy" breed. Its development sprang from need and even to-day in its native country it performs many practical functions.

The earliest history of horses on the Iberian peninsula is, of course, obscured by time and lack of records. Many Spanish historians claim there were horses in Spain before the great land bridge that linked the Iberian peninsula with the African mainland became submerged under the sea, and therefore it is a mistake to think of the horses as being introduced at a later date by man. Nevertheless, Spain was a much invaded and conquered country, and over hundreds of years a succession of occupying armies introduced horses in great numbers. Certainly the great Hasdrubal of Carthage is recorded as importing two thousand Numidian mares. These horses were reputed to be "as fast as wind", and it is likely that from this influx might be seen the beginnings of an emergent type.

The Romans invaded Spain in 200 B.C. and tamed the wild horses. They also inevitably brought fresh stock to the peninsula. When the Romans retreated these horses would have been left to run wild again and breed with little interference from humans. All grazing animals evolve under the influence of the terrain in which they live. The vast hinterland of Spain offers a variety of landscape, but in many areas a soil structure and climate exists which is markedly different from that of its neighbouring countries. Cut off from the north by the vast ranges of the Pyrenees and from the south by the straits of Gibraltar, it can be assumed that over the centuries which elapsed between the introduction of the Numidian horses and the coming of the Vandal hordes from the North, the horse in Iberia evolved along lines that would make it recognisably different from the horse from different climates. We live in a time when communications have made regional differences less significant than they used to be. However, one only has to look at the variety of breeds of sheep that developed after the Agrarian revolution in England to see what great local variety in breed type resulted from sheep staying for generations on one type of soil, and to realise that the Spanish landscape would assist the evolvement of a type of horse best suited to survive there.

A young foal at a stud farm in Andalucia looks out to a life as one of the local aristocrats of the horse world.

Photo: Judy Blake

The great migrations from the north started with the coming of the Vandals, those Teutonic conquerors who reached Spain in the fourth century A.D. The Vandals brought with them fresh influxes of horses but now a slightly taller, stouter animal from Germany, which in turn interbred with the more slightly built indigenous horse. The Vandals were succeeded by the Visigoths and during this dark period it is improbable that any organised selective breeding for domestic horses took place. However, each succeeding wave of newcomers must have had some influence on the breed.

In the eighth century occurred the greatest civilising force in Spanish history. The Muslim invasion of 711 A.D. brought to the Iberian peninsula a people who combined religion, heart and a vigorous aesthetic sense to a degree not equalled again until the Italian renaissance of the 15th century. Their rule in Southern Spain was to last 800 years and when they were finally driven out they left behind them a legacy of great cities and architecture which still stands to-day. All over the south of Spain, the traveller can still see signs of the Moorish occupation and a visit to the Great Mosque at Cordoba is sufficient to convince the modern tourist of the grandeur of their architecture. The Moors, of course, brought with them horses, this time the Arabian and the Barb. The Muslim influence on the Spanish horse is difficult to calculate since the Emirs bred their Arab and Barb horses in stables devoted to these breeds and were not keen on intermixing with the local horses they found on their arrival. However, it is not uncommon to hear of Emirs' stables which held two thousand animals and it seems inconceivable that some of this Arab

Waiting to receive the 'Champion of Champions' award at the culmination of the 1989 Jerez Feria. This stallion, the property of Snr. Diosdada, shows all the dignity and calmness that characterizes the breed!

Photo: Judy Blake

blood failed to intermingle with the Spanish horse, although some Spanish historians are proud of claiming that the Andalucian of today is free of Arab blood. If the Moors had little influence on the Spanish horse by breeding, they had a very great influence for other reasons.

The Christian armies had until now used the horse as a method of transport and for hauling wagons. Where actual cavalry was used it tended to be ponderous, relying on heavy armour, which in turn required a heavy horse. It was not very long before sufficient painful experience had taught the Christian monarchs that they were no match for the lighter agile Arab horseman. The Moors were literally able to "run rings round" the Christian cavalry, and darting in and out could strike and disable the enemy who were unable to manoeuvre fast enough to take avoiding action, let alone mete out the same treatment. In this lesson lay probably the greatest single influence on the development of the modern Spanish horse. The Spanish kings soon started selective breeding in order to develop a smaller more agile horse, which would enable them to compete with the Moorish cavalry. By the eleventh century, the Spanish calvalry horse had become a fighting animal and not just a means of transport. The movements required by cavalry men who wished to come out of these skirmishes victorious (or at least alive) were complex and the horse was no longer a moving seat from which the rider might parry and thrust, but rather a partner in a life or death venture.

Out of this cauldron emerged the great fighting movements that would later become enshrined in classical high school dressage.

Mares and young stock drink in the river at their breeding stud. Foals spend their early days running free with their mothers and some of the bigger ranches have quite large herds of pure bred Andalucians.

Photo:

The Capriole, the Courbet, and the Levade were not just formalised movements for the entertainment of spectators but rather those necessary manoeuvres by which a horse could protect its rider and even execute aggressive acts. Such movements required the greatest agility, the ability to perform rapid sideways movements and to lower the quarters and switch the centre of gravity on command. To achieve this, much selective breeding was necessary and the Spanish produced by the eleventh century a horse which enabled their cavalry to compete on equal terms with Muslims.

The Spanish horse became justly famous during these wars and after the Moors were driven from Spain, the Spanish Kings continued to further the breed. Today we speak of the Andalucian horse, when perhaps we should refer to the Spanish horse, but nowhere in Spain was so suitable to the development of this magnificent breed as the district of Andalucia. Here the great studs developed and in 1571 Philip the Second started a royal stud at Cordoba and opened a stud book. With the country on a war footing, great inducements had been offered to those who would breed this animal, and taxes and privileges were given to the larger breeders. By the sixteenth century, the Andalucian had become more than just a cavalry horse, it had become a status symbol. The finest examples were eagerly acquired by other countries, and kings had their portraits painted mounted on these magnificent animals. Royal interest and patronage, and the development of studs by the Spanish aristocracy was a highly significant factor in the breed's progress.

However, Kings come and go, and

Many bullfighting horses receive injuries, and this picture shows why. All the manoeuvres have to place the rider within range of the bull and this inevitably leads to very close 'brushes' with the bull. Here it seems the bull must injure the horse but in fact the movement was successful and the horse avoided real contact.

Photo: Judy Blake

aristocratic families do not always maintain a policy from one generation to another; therefore, variations in regional types might be expected along with variations of taste and preference. In the fifteenth century there occurred what is probably the greatest single influence on the breed as it is known today. The Carthusian monks entered the world of horse breeding and took up the task of improving the Andalucian with a fervour and dedication which is awe inspiring.

When St. Bruno of Cologne founded the monastic order in the mountains of Chartreuse, near Grenoble, France, he could not have foreseen that centuries later the order would be best known for the production of the world famous Chartreuse Liqueur, which is its major source of revenue. He might well, and with some justification, have felt that this was a trivialising label with which to tag one of the great religious orders of the world. Even stranger perhaps is that this semi solitary and purely contemplative order should become the saviour and mainstay of the Andalucian horse.

All breed societies know that a stud book is an essential for the maintaining of purity in a breed. When Philip the Second opened the first stud book, he started the breeding programme on a course designed to fix the standard for the future. Unfortunately, the Royal stud along with other great studs suffered from unfortunate innovators in later generations. Not all keepers of the Royal Stud maintained the pure blood lines, and in some cases breeding took place with animals outside the stud books with unfortunate consequences. The Carthusians, however, brought to the business of breeding horses the single-minded discipline that might be

This three-year old colt from the Cortijo Olivera will turn a lighter grey as it ages.
It is one of the young stock destined to pull a carriage in a team.
Although primarily trained for carriage work, the young horses at the Olivera Stud also receive training for ridden horses.

Photo: Judy Blake

expected from a monastic order. In 1476 the Carthusians received a gift of ten thousand acres of land in Jerez and from then on the great wealth of the church was available to aid the breeding programme. So fanatical were the monks in their zeal for purity that more than one breeder who swayed from the rigid line was threatened with excommunication. While the policies of other studs varied as succeeding generations took over control, the rigidity of the Carthusian programme was such as to provide the back-bone and continuity of the pure Andalucian horse.

The success of the breed, its outstanding beauty and flamboyant paces sometimes posed a threat to its future. When the French occupied Spain during the Napoleonic period the best of the Andalucian horses were among the treasures pillaged from the country. Somehow the Carthusians managed to protect enough pure breds to enable the breed to continue after the occupation. These precious blood lines plus some which, remarkably, survived the depredations of the occupying forces were all that remained available to the breeders in Spain in the 19th Century. Here again we see the remarkable resilience of the Carthusian Order who continued throughout to devote their efforts to the preservation of this quite remarkable animal. By the middle of the 19th Century the Royal studs were flourishing again and at this point the Carthusians rather surprisingly diverged from the other breeders. They continued in their efforts to produce the pure horse, but succeeded in developing a slightly heavier type, and the visitor to modern-day Spanish studs may be slightly surprised to hear reference to a "Cartagenan" horse or as

Acoso y Derribo. The moment of the knockdown shown here by Don Alvaro Domecq.
A clean knock-over is the aim of the rider, and in a competition marks will be lost if more than one attempt has to be made.
When testing young stock for suitabililty as potential fighting bulls the animal is bowled over until it turns on its tormentors. It is than graded for its courage and resistance to this treatment.

Photo:

we sometimes call it the Carthusian horse. This is a slightly heavier type although this is not to imply any coarseness. Its proponents claim for it a greater hardiness and believe it to be superior to the slightly more delicate and lighter Andalucian that has been developed in other studs.

By the end of the nineteenth century, the age of the horse as a universal haulage animal and a vital element in the fighting capability of all armies was over. The introduction of the combustion engine spelt the end of the horse in its traditional role. The Battle of Omdhurman at the end of the nineteenth century saw the last true cavalry charge, and although vast numbers of horses were used in France during the Great War, by 1918 the lorry and the tank had taken over. The future of the military horse was from now on to be strictly ceremonial. In Spain, the control of breeding was in the hands of the military, and this illustration of the horse's military origins continues to the present time. The Spanish Government controls the breeding standards through the military stud, and although there are many fine private studs in Spain today, stallions are passed for breeding purposes by officials of the Criadores de Caballos under the control of the army cavalry wing.

Cross country carriage driving is a popular sport in Andalucia. This is an established sport which can produce spectacular moments that thrill spectators. The Spanish personality often adds an extra touch of 'Machismo' to the skills of the whip. In this photograph a team enters the water at a ford in great style and at speed.

Photo:

2.

Dressage

". . .the noblest horse in the world, fittest of all for a king in the day of Triumph." These words by the Duke of Newcastle (1592—1676) illustrate the position of the Andalucian in the horse riding hierarchy in the seventeeth century.

Up to the middle of the eighteenth century it was indisputably the first horse of Europe. Today, it is often described as "ideal for Haute Ecole." And yet it has failed to emerge successfully into the modern international dressage arena. Why is this so? Why is a breed so involved with the origins of dressage and its developement during the sixteenth, seventeenth and eighteenth centuries now regarded as removed from the mainstream of international competition? Clearly some great change has taken place to bring about this shift in emphasis.

Has the breed changed or has dressage developed along different paths? To answer this, it is perhaps necessary to look at the emergence of modern competition dressage and the way the demands on the horse have changed.

Classical dressage evolved in a logical manner from the needs of the cavalry. To be successful, a cavalry charge against trained and resolute infantry called for disciplined riders on well-trained horses. This seems an obvious enough fact to anyone who rides or in any way deals with horses. However, we live in an age which is comparatively remote from the horse and Hollywood has turned out a great number of films showing cavalry warfare as an undisciplined and spectacular display of rough riding and sheer speed. Of course speed was part of the psychological

A young rider makes 'shoulder-in' on this bay Andalucian. Sideways, or lateral, movements are very natural to the breed which although often criticized for lack of impulsion is extremely easy to train for all lateral work. The so-called failure to find forward impulsion is really a matter of training techniques rather than any breed characteristic. There is an increasing interest in Spain directed towards modern competition dressage and the results are proving that Andalucians can complete F.E.I dressage tests with great facility.

Photo:

shock produced by cavalry assault, but it was seldom more than a part of the whole. The main objects of any cavalry rider were to be effective at the end of the approach and to be able to survive to return to his own ranks. These aims called for a high degree of skill on the part of both rider and horse.

As cavalry warfare developed so did the need to weld individuals into regulated and disciplined units. Cavalry schools developed and horses were taught to execute manoeuvres useful to the rider during the cut and thrust of engagement. Gradually these movements became standardised and many of them survive today within classical dressage.

At the highest level of training the horse became the partner of his rider and not just a means to get to and from the battle. Horses were taught to jump in the air, to kick out with their hind legs at the enemy, to rear on command, and to change pace and direction at their rider's signals. Here may be revognised the 'Capriole', the 'Levade' and the pirouette of 'Haute Ecole'.

Running parallel to the development of the trained cavalry mount was the growth in interest in the art of riding by the aristocracy and landed classes. From Roman times the upper classes had dominated the arts in general and horsemanship was considered one of the preserves of gentlemen. The Romans themselves even went so far as to refer to the 'equestrian order', thus implying that a mounted man was superior to the plebeian masses,—as in those days he undoubtedly was. Raising everyday activity to art form was part of the philosophy of the great Renaissance. After the darkness that fell on European civilization following the fall

'Doma Vaquera'. In the sequence illustrated (from right to left) the rider asks his horse to come to halt from fast canter or gallop. The movement corresponds with 'canter to halt' in competition dressage. The marks awarded for this movement are given according to the speed and rhythm of the canter and the number of strides needed to come to halt. Frequently, the horse sits on its haunches into a sliding halt.

Photo: Judy Blake

of the Roman empire came the great re-birth of excellence in all things that, appropriately enough, had its beginnings in fourteenth century Italy.

We are accustomed to referring to the Renaissance as a period of re-birth and flowering for learning and the arts. This is a simplification of the immense upheaval that occurred over two centuries. Humanism arose as a way of thinking, at first alongside and later somewhat opposing traditional religious thought. Out of the humanist movement there naturally arose a belief in the merit of individual expertise. The 'complete' man of the Renaissance arrived. Art was seen as existing in everything a sixteenth century gentleman occupied himself with. No longer confined to painting, poetry and prose, it was seen in other everyday activities. Horse riding was certainly in the forefront. After all, wasn't it a skill elevated to art by the Greek General and philosopher Xenophon?

In a specializing age we read with astonishment of the omnicompetence of Renaissance man. Men like Alberti (1404—1472) whose extraordinary physical feats included springing over a man's head with his feet together, desired above all to appear faultless to others in three things, in walking, in speaking and in riding. In Mantua, Francesco Gonzaga founded the Mantuan Stud from which came the infallible winners of the horse races that were starting up in all the major towns of the peninsula. The stud at Mantua kept stallions and mares from Spain and provided a steady stream of the best cavalry chargers.

The Renaissance was not confined to Italy and its influence spread even to insular

The author's stallion 'Cariolo III' was bred by Snr. Guadiola and first trained by Mercedes Gonzolez.

He later completed his training with Luis Ramos Paul at Los Palacios.

Arriving in the Channel Islands in 1985 he returned to Spain for a short spell but finally went back again to Guernsey, where he died of cancer, aged 11 years, in 1989.

'Cariola' was very typical of the lighter type of Andalucian, and enjoyed the breed's ability to learn very quickly the more advanced classical movements.

Photo: Judy Blake

communities such as England. By the seventeenth century England produced one of the great riding masters of all time, the Duke of Newcastle.

Other great European Masters such as Gueriniere arose and great riding academies were founded by gifted teachers who furthered the art of Haute Ecole and took the old cavalry movements to set them into a body of work universally taken up by other academies.

At this stage national differences were not really in existence. The historical development of the art of riding shows that, stimulated by the flowering of this art in Europe, from the sixteenth century onwards riding academics were founded in many different countries and the European gentry studied at the famous riding schools under the great teachers of the time and strove to perfect the standards.

Therefore up to the end of the nineteenth century all riding instruction came down from common sources. We can see clearly that the art of riding and horse training had by this time long been crystallised into a compendium of movements and changes of pace which at the highest level of achievement was 'Haute Ecole'. The ability to excel at Haute Ecole was predominantly present in the Andalucian horse and its closest decendent, the Lippizaner.

The end of the Great War saw a change in the horse's role. No longer a staple part of all transport the horse was in future to fulfill leisure and ceremonial roles in all but the most unmechanised communities.

Dressage was no longer to be the preserve of the few who studied in the rather monastic atmosphere of the great riding

There are black stallions among the breed, but they are unusual. This fine example shows the glossy coat and proud carriage of the Andalucian, the black colouring adding a dramatic dimension.

Photo: Judy Blake

YUMBO

academies. Before the century was very old other nations and continents entered the field of international competition, and as the aeroplane and railway shrank the world's distances, the sport of riding and dressage became universal.

In any great expansion new and vigorous opinions came to challenge the old established ways. Dressage was to prove no exception. New nations, arriving on the competition scene, formed their own national associations and regulating bodies. Nationally appointed judges brought from their emergent countries new and sometimes conflicting standards. In 1921 the Federation Equestre Internationale (F E I) was founded. The F E I promotes and regulates the sport of riding throughout the world and puts a global stamp on an art which was for a long time the exclusive preserve of civilised Europe. Dressage Tests of different levels, representing different stages in the horse's level of training, were devised and published by the different national dressage bodies, and F E I Tests followed for use in international competitions.

The classical movements became modified by the demands of modern life. The 'airs off the ground' where the trainer, using long reins, stands on the ground controlling the horse's movements showing off such spectacular airs as the 'Capriole', 'Levade' and 'Courbet' are now only part of the display given by schools of equitation deriving from older times and traditions. The mounted version of these movements has suffered a similar fate and is not part of any dressage competition, international or otherwise. They are still to be seen in the displays by the Spanish Riding School of

'Haragan', a very good example of the breed, ridden by Ricardo Donoso. 'Haragan' was brought to England by his owner Mrs. Gill Warrilow but returned to Spain when Mr. & Mrs. Warrilow returned there to live. 'Haragan' carries the brand of Don Salvador Garcia of Fuengirola.

Photo: Judy Blake

Vienna and the Cadre Noir Cavalry School at Saumur, France. Portugal and Spain keep these classical airs alive and a visitor to Jerez in Andalucia can watch performances given to the public by the Escuela del Arte Equestre, founded and headed by Alvarez Domecq.

In this environment the Andalucian, with its short back, the ability to lower its hindquarters and its amazing agility reigns supreme as does its offshoot, the Lippizaner in Vienna and its other derivative, the Lusitano in Portugal.

In one sense, however, the training and performances at these great schools have developed in isolation. Or perhaps it is more true to say that they continue the classical teachings regarded as universal up to this century. In the modern dressage arena there are now significant differences in the way some movements are performed. An example of this is the movement of 'shoulder-in'. Some riders and teachers resist admitting to any differences that are significant but the 'shoulder-in' ridden in modern dressage tests is performed with the front quarters and shoulder at less severe an angle from the track or wall than its ancestor, the classical 'shoulder-in'. There is a greater emphasis on forward movement and metronomic regularity of pace driven by powerful hindquarters which endow each pace with great 'volume'. Within the last thirty years international judges have preferred the big striding horses from the north, Hanoverian, Dutch and Swedish horses which display a different movement from that of the smaller, more agile breeds. Olympic Gold Medals have been the preserve of this type of horse and however much the spectators may delight

The mane and tail of the Andalucian stallion is its crown and glory. When young the mane is 'hogged' to strengthen future growth. Thereafter, mane trimming or pulling is not done, as the quality of the mane is a source of pride. The illustration shows an extreme example which is hardly typical. The mane and tail shown here have grown to unusual length and attracted a lot of attention in the parade at the 1989 Feria in Jerez.

Photo: Ingrid Telford

in the light dancing steps of the smaller horses, such as those from Russia, the F E I judges have not favoured them. Certainly the Andalucian, with its showy front action and short hind action is not going to find favour in this area of competition.

If there is any one towering figure in the world of Haute Ecole who seems to straddle the two eras, it must be Alois Podhajsky, Director of the Spanish riding School in Vienna between 1939 and 1965, a period of enormous significance in the School's long history. Colonel Podhajsky died in 1972 and his last published work 'The Art of Dressage' was just completed. It is remarkble for its clarity and perspective.

In the book Podhajsky enumerates the requirements of the dressage arena according to the principles of classical riding. These requirements are the same for modern competition as for the classical Haute Ecole and take no account of the vogue for big Germanic horses.

Although Colonel Podhajsky was dealing in the book with the competition world as he saw it, his list of requirements come straight from the classical world and the schools of Vienna and Jerez.

He named six main principles as follows:

1. A straight horse going forward with impulsion.

2. Absolute purity of the paces and regularity of the steps. These convey beauty to the riding horse and may truly be called the music of movement.

3. The horse should accept the bit with calmness and confidence and submit willingly and spontaneously to the

Luis Ramos Paul, one of Spain's most successful trainers, schooling the bay stallion 'Vittorioso' belonging to Miss Marilyn Tennent. Marilyn Tennent is one of the foremost authorities on the Andalucian and its blood lines and spends much of her time working with Luis Ramos at his Los Palacios establishment.

Photo: Judy Blake

guidance of his rider. It is the horse that should seek this guidance. On no account should the rider force the horse into a determined position of head and neck by means of the reins. Collection obtained in this incorrect manner is invariably betrayed by the lack of freedom of the paces.

4. Suppleness of the horse must have been obtained and improved by logically built in gymnastic training. It is reflected in the smoothness of the movements, in fluent transitions and last but not least, in the absolute balance in all exercises. This balance can be obtained only when sufficient energy is present in the hindquarters of the horse, which take their full or greater share in carrying the rider's weight. When the horse moves in this manner, he conveys the impression that, in terms of mechanics, the motor as the source of movement is located in the hind quarters and its driving power is guided and regulated by the reins in the rider's hands.

5. The horse's physical proficiency is mainly the result of his suppleness provided there are absolute physical self-control and perfect balance. It is manifested in the correctness of the exercises with regards to the sequence of the steps as well as the preciseness of figures. This adroitness should become obvious in any phase of the test, not only in the difficult movements of the more advanced classes but also in the collected paces and in the performance of single exercises such as voltes and halts.

Many trainers use long reining as a basis for schooling horses, but this rider long reins while mounted. This method is not as uncommon in Spain as it is in more northerly Europe.

Photo:

X

6. The horse's obedience, the most important requirement of a dressage horse, is mentioned last for a good reason. Obedience is the logical result of the above-mentioned requirements having been fulfilled. It must never be that of a drilled poodle. It should be the proud achievement of gymnastic training of the horse based on preservation of his willingness and individuality.

A young stallion of light build belonging to Snr. Romero Benitez.

Photo:

Thus one of the great masters of riding who might be seen to span two disciplines makes it clear there is only one. If we accept that the training techniques for both classical and modern competition dressage are the same, and the basic principles of movement in the horse do not differ, then the reason for the Andalucian's absence from mainstream competition must lie elsewhere. As has been stated, fashion undoubtedly plays a part. It is very likely, however, that another cause is the development of Spanish riding in a vacuum away from other Western countries.

Spain still remains a largely rural economy and in Andalucia the horse is strongly linked to the soil. Unlike other more northerly countries which are now heavily industrialised, and where the horse is mainly a part of the sport and leisure activity, Spain still uses the horse for many of its day to day tasks. Its part in the life of the great bull ranches equates more with the life of the American Western horse than a European riding horse.

In England, for instance, the average rider trains his horse, if he trains it at all, to be traffic proof and to be a suitable general purpose hack. Whatever the degree of training it is mostly to the precepts of the

British Horse Society, where instructors are the only recognised professional teachers available to the student. Therefore if a horse receives training the teaching follows a common policy.

This is not so in Spain, where there are different schools of thought and very different methods used to train the horses. On the ranches, where the horse has a job of work to perform, rough and ready means of early training are often used. Horses are often broken with the spike on the underside of the noseband, the 'filete', a thin wire-like bit, and very sharp spurs. The rationale for these methods is that the young horse learns quickly to obey its rider, the short sharp shock being a salutary lesson not to disobey. Supporters of these training methods point to what they see as the average rider in other countries sawing at his horse's mouth and pummelling its flanks with unspurred legs when the horse is fully mature and point out that horses trained with the apparently severe methods while young do not have to endure this kind of prolonged treatment.

It is certainly true that horses trained with spiked noseband stop 'on a sixpence' at the slightest pressure of the rider's rein finger. It is equally certain, however, that the horse trained in this manner will have a lifetime reluctance to go forward 'into the bridle'. These methods promote instant obedience learnt early and for the busy vaquero provide an acceptable solution. It must be said that the method does not in any way impede the horse's agility, and its agility to turn on its haunches and to move sideways at will is not impaired in any way.

The calls of the ranch work, the often dangerous work of bull and cow testing,

Although many think of the Andalucian breed as typified by grey, or 'white', horses, there are many bay Andalucians. This young stallion, in a distracted moment, shows the noble profile and fine coat so typical of this breed.

Photo:

require great riding skills as well as sure footed and agile horses. The natural extension of this is the rejoneador, the mounted bull fighter. In this branch of bull fighting the horse has to work with a fast and dangerous bull within the small confines of the bullring. Here great speed in a straight line over a measured distance is useless. The horses used by the rejoneador have to be brave and highly skilled. The rider's performance, and his life, will depend on the sure footed agility and balance of his mount.

So we see that harsh methods, with harsh bitting and sharp spurs, do not impair balance, and agility. To see the Spanish 'garrochistas' (bull testers) and rejoneadors at work is to see riding of the highest degree of skill and control.

Naturally the riders themselves are proud of their skills and show them off in competitions. These competitons are held all over Southern Spain, sometimes at the ferias and sometimes in conjunction with dressage competitions. The discipline of 'country riding' known as 'Doma Vaquera' is often more popular than dressage, or 'Doma Classica' because it shows the most spectacular movements which appeal to the spectators. Nevertheless Doma Vaquera riding has a place in the dressage spectrum and many of the compulsory movements that have to be included in the rider's programme are drawn from the requirements of the ranch, formalised and presented to the judges for their verdict. In this we can see the same progress as happened centuries earlier when the battle training became formalised into what we now call dressage.

The Doma Vaquera tests contain much that is instantly recognisable to the dressage rider.

A typical Andalucian head, mane plaited, ready for driving.

Photo: Jancos

Instant halt from canter, flying change of leg in canter and pirouette are all performed. If similarities are present, so too are profound differences, mostly lying in the manner of performance. The halt from canter is a sudden affair involving going froward at great speed, then a sliding halt often involving the horse sitting on its haunches. Movements such as pirouette are performed to display the horse's ability to turn quickly and no account is taken of maintaining the rhythm and beat of the hind legs as is required in dressage.

Doma Vaquera competitions are often staged at the same time as Doma Classica events. It is quite usual for riders to compete in both disciplines. Some of Spain's most respected dressage riders and trainers have strong connections with country riding.

Luis Ramos Paul, former country riding champion of Spain, is a highly successful and skilled dressage trainer. Perhaps the interrelation between Doma Vaquera and Doma Classica is best illustrated by the dominant figure of Alvaro Domecq. A member of the Domecq Sherry family, Alvaro followed the family bullfighting tradition. Many members of the family were and are rejoneadors. Alvaro, over many years, became such a popular hero of the bullring that when he gave his farewell performance Spanish television covered the event and many spectators became extremely emotional. Yet Alvaro Domecq also founded the Escuela del Arte Esquestre in Jerez and is still seen leading the classical quadrille and performing the airs off the ground.

It may well be this dichotomy of outlook that partly explains why it has not been a major force in international dressage.

'Guadalimar', the stud stallion of Senor Francisco Olivera. The Olivera stud produces many fine horses which reflect the owner's interest in 'enganches', the carriage driving which is so popular in this part of Spain. 'Guadalimar' has been 'Champion of Champions' twice at the Feria del Caballos, Jerez.

Photo: Judy Blake

3

Bullfighting on Horseback

The Andalucian horse still enjoys a strong position in the country life of Southern Spain. Its amazing agility and gentle temperament make it ideal for working cattle and its sure-footedness enables it to cope with hilly and sometimes mountainous terrain.

Andalucia is a predominantly agrarian province, and everyone's existence is touched by the tradition of the country's rural life. In Spain, particularly in the South, the bullfight still enjoys great popularity. Every provincial town of any note has its bullring and there are 'corridas' held regularly throughout the season. The bullfight is a force in Spanish life and a strong influence on training and development of the modern andalucian breed.

The famous philosopher Jose Ortigay Gasset wrote "Since 1740 the bullfight has occupied a permanent position in 'Spanish Life', for example, in Ferdinand VI's reign, Caripillo, a prominent offical, wrote that he was very concerned because men in Saragossa were pawning their shirts in order to pay to see the bullfight. It is quite obvious, in fact, as I have established with careful research, that Spanish history since 1650 at least, cannot be understood without reference to it. One has to know a lot to understand what a bullfighter really is and he who does, will understand some of the fundamentals of our modern history."

The origins of bullfighting are lost in antiquity. Bullfighting on horse back is certainly referred to in many ancient chronicles and reference is made to the old bullring in Madrid being built in the reign of

Although there are many modern bullrings there are still more built in the days when architecture in Spain was courtly and grand in style. The Plaza del Toros in Seville is a magnificent arena which provides an impressive setting for the 'corrida'.
A packed crowd watches enthralled by the horsemanship of the rejoneador, Javier Buendia, on a horse belonging to Snr. Benitez Cubero of Seville.

Photo:

John II of Trastamara (1406—1454). The popularity of bullfighting flourished with the growth of equitation as an art and went hand in hand with the notions of courtly chivalry which were developing at the same time.

In these early days bullfighting on horseback was only for gentlemen. The commonalty only provided spectators. The mounted gentleman was attended by servants on foot whose job was to assist their master should he lose his spear or his horse be gored by the bull.

In 1700 the Bourbon Monarch, Philip V ascended the Spanish throne and his dislike of bullfighting caused the nobility to abandon the sport. It was during this period that the bullfighter on foot appeared. The common classes took to appearing in the bullring and the matador of to-day was born. By 1830 a Royal School of Bullfighting was founded at Seville.

Following the decline of bullfighting on horseback as the favourite sport of the Spanish nobility, two centuries passed before it was popularised again. It did however remain a favourite pastime for Portuguese riders. Earlier this century Antonio Canero introduced the riding style of Andalucia to the bullring with sensational results. His popularity with the crowds led to the re-establishment of the 'Rejoneador', the mounted bullfighter.

It was not too difficult for the horseman to rejoin the bullfighting scene. Much of the skill required is necessarily present in the horsemen and horses who work with the bulls on the ranches. The lance or its day to day counterpart the 'garrocha' or blunted pole, is normally part of working with cattle in the Andalucian countryside. The spanish

It is vital that a rejoneador's horse is agile and has the ability to show rapid changes of pace. The timing needed to cross the path of the charging bull while avoiding contact with its horns is very precise and the horse must respond totally and immediately to the slightest signal from the rider.

Photo: Judy Blake

cattle worker is accustomed to using the pole as part of his daily work both as an implement to help him separate animals from one another and a defence against aggressive cattle.

On the ranches where fighting bulls are bred it is customary to test the young bulls to assess their fitness to eventually take part in a 'corrida'. The breeder also wants to select bulls for breeding which have the characteristics required of a 'Toro Bravo' or fighting bull. Cows must also be tested since they also will pass on through their genes their own characteristics.

Aggression and courage are the qualities looked for. The bull calf is first tested before it reaches two years of age.

The calf is separated from the herd and two riders carrying long wooden poles give chase. The rider who is on the right hand side aims his pole at the fleeing calf's hind quarters and knocks him over. This procedure is repeated until the calf turns on its tormentors and gives chase. According to how long it takes for the calf to become aggressor it is graded in the record book. Next, a rider is stationed near the angry calf on a heavily padded horse. If the calf is brave it will readily charge horse and rider. The rider fends it off with a long pointed pole and finally administers a wound to its shoulder.

This type of testing, a typically Andalucian method, involves great skill by the horseman taking part. It also requires highly trained horses who respond immediately to their rider's commands, and who have no fear of cattle.

The riders who work with the long poles (garrochas) are know as 'garrochistas'. So

After a successful placing of the banderilla, the rider accelerates away from the bull, who only manages to reach the horse's tail.

Photo: Judy Blake

skilful do they become that competitions are held all over Andalucia. In these competitions the garrochistas display their skills and horsemanship. These riders take part in the Doma Vaquera dressage competitions as well.

If the work on the ranches and in the bullrings requires bull and riders, the third element which must be present is the highly skilled horse. To see the Andalucian horse at work, whether bull testing, in dressage, or competition bull fighting, is to see a display of agility and obedience that cannot be described by words alone. In this environment the horse echoes its glories of past centuries. The mount of kings, it today carries the rejoneador, the mounted bullfighter, who is a king in Spain today, whatever the feeling of the anti-bullfighter lobby.

The great rejoneador Alvaro Domecq Romero, typifies the combined riding skills that may be found in Andalucia. A member of the great Domecq Sherry family and son of Alvarez Domecq, a past master of bullfighting on horse back, Alvero has for many years been the hero of the bullring. Perhaps more important he founded the famous riding school, El Escuela del Arte Equestre, that is now the accepted centre of classical riding in Spain. Situated in Jerez the school is built in the grounds of the old royal palace and takes students from all over Spain. Foreign students also graduate there and are taught classical dressage on pure bred Andalucian horses.

The Jerez school, like its counterpart, the Spanish riding school in Vienna, travels the world giving demonstrations of the classical movements and includes in its programme

If you are in Jerez, you are likely to notice plenty of evidence of the Domecq family influence. Don Alvaro Domecq, rejoneador and classical trainer, is seen here at the ringside at the Jerez Plaza de Toros. His appearance always causes interest, and he is greatly respected by the current bullfighters.

Photo: Judy Blake

the musical quadrille. There is also a performance given weekly at the Jerez school and people travel great distances to enjoy a truly spectacular display. Domecq himself often appears at these perfomances as lead rider and also demonstrates the classical airs off the ground.

The Domecq ranch breeds fighting bulls as well as pure bred Andalucian horses. Famous for both, the family exerts great influence on the performance and development of the pure bred horse in Spain today.

On previous page:

A group of riders waiting their turn to display their skills at 'Acoso y Derribo', literally, chase and knockdown.
This way of testing stock to see if the animals have the qualities required for the bullring is also used as a display of riding skills.
The riders work in pairs, chasing the young bull when it is released, and knocking it down by prodding, and unbalancing it, with the long pole. The rider on the right hand side does the pole work, the left hand rider is there as support and prevents the bull from turning out of the line of run.

The rejoneador will, when possible, make the kill from horseback. If he has to dismount, the horse must not hinder him, and this horse, his rider having dismounted, leaves the bullring on his own.

4
Spanish Riding School in Jerez

The Andalucian Breed certainly suffered a decline in fortune during this century, but in recent years it has made great strides towards recovering its popularity.

This recovery may be attributed to a number of contributary factors, not least the enormous popularity of post-war Spain as a holiday centre for Europeans. Perhaps the most perfect setting for the breed is in its native environment.

Certainly the success of the Spanish Tourist Industry has meant more and more people becoming familiar with Spain. For many years, the visitors were more or less confined to the coasts. Poor roads, package holiday arrangements, and time factors meant Spain was, for many people, magnificent if crowded beaches with almost guaranteed sunshine. Even the rapidly improving road system did little more than open up the principle cities to tourism. Indeed, better roads often reduce the visitor's likehood of visiting anywhere not on the actual main routes.

Nevertheless, it was inevitable that sooner or later, in a world becoming increasingly affluent and sophisticated in travel matters, the tourists would start to discover the interior of this truly beautiful country. Once into the countryside of Andalucia, one is in the heartland of the Pure Bred horse. A large majority of the studs belonging to members of the Breeders' Association are situated here. This land is the land of the 'Toro Bravo', the fighting bull.

A drive through Andalucia will take the visitor through the great cattle farms and ranches that predominate in the rolling

A rider of the Escuela of Jerez warms up his horse before joining his fellows for the classical quadrille to music. The Escuela is built in the grounds of the old royal palace, and visitors may see the riders of the school practising outside.

Photo:

countryside. Many of the studs and yeguadas, the breeding herds of pure-bred mares, are contained within the cattle ranches. Many of these ranches also specialize in the breeding of fighting bulls.

Few visitors to this part of Spain fail to visit the magnificent city of Seville. With its glorious architecture and avenues. Seville is an almost mandatory stopping place for the tourist, whether by car or coach. Seville is full of history and the old city with its 'Jewish quarter' is not to be missed.

Indeed, Seville is full of so many attractions, which include some of the best fish restaurants in southern Spain, that many visitors seem to forget that only an hour away on the new motorway link is the town of Jerez de la Frontera, the very centre of the Sherry industry. Here, for centuries, the great Sherry houses have owned their 'bodegas' and produced the wine which takes its name from the town, It is also the international centre of the Andalucian Pure Bred horse.

The usual way to reach Jerez is by the road leading from the coast between Algeciras and Gibraltar. This is because most visitors to Spain still stay on the coast. The enormous amount of hotel and villa development there makes it the most convenient place to find accommodation, sufficient for the hundreds of thousands of tourists, who come here each year.

Shortly after leaving the coast the road runs through the town of Los Barrios, and Jerez is some ninety minutes' drive away. It runs through fighting bull country and the road is named 'Ruta de Toros', route of the bulls. So typical of Spain, the moment Los Barrios is left behind, you seem to enter a world remote from holiday resorts and

Don Alvaro Domecq, director of the Royal School, prepares to lead his riders into the indoor school at Jerez for a public exhibition of classical dressage. The school gives public displays each week which show the work done at the school and includes the classical movements and 'airs off the ground'. These shows, given to music, are very popular with both tourists and local Spaniards. Whenever possible Alvaro Domecq leads the quadrille in the displays by the school which is itself a monument to his influence on Spanish horsemanship.

Photo:

tourists, a large area of gently rolling countryside, cork trees, arable land and cattle ranches. On either side, small mountain towns with ancient monasteries and fortifications are reminders of links with the medieval past.

Nearing Jerez, vineyards become more obvious and the distinctive soil that produces the sherry grape.

Quite suddenly, there is a view of the beautiful structure of the Carthusian Monastery that dominates the entry into the town. Those who understand the history of the Spanish Pure Bred will acknowledge the huge debt owed by the Breed to the Carthusians. Their enthusiasm and dedication to the breed, their strict adherance and attention to bloodlines in the early days of development of the breed as we know it today, endows the monastery with something of the quality of a shrine to lovers of Andalucian horses. It is also a sign that you are only a few kilometres from the town of Jerez, the modern day 'Mecca' for owners and breeders who wish to see for themselves the centre of activity for the promotion of the breed.

Unlike Seville, Jerez has been relatively untouched by the tourist. It remains a working town with limited facilities for visitors wishing to stay there. It is therefore more likely to see tourists who come there for the day.

There are two main hotels currently available, both situated on the Avenida Alvarez Domecq. They offer a choice of extremely modern, international style facilities, with more typically Spanish surroundings at the Jerez Hotel. The visitor arriving in Jerez before eleven o'clock in the

This study of a stallion (the mount of Alvaro Domecq) at the Jerez School shows the outline so typical of this breed. Those familiar with the Lippizaner horses of Vienna will recognise the similarities between the breeds.
The Lippizaner is the direct descendant of the Andalucian.

Photo:

morning would miss part of the local flavour if he did not take a coffee and 'churros', a delicious and light piece of confectionery often described as a type of doughnut, but in fact much lighter and less sweet, traditional Andalucian accompaniment to morning coffee.

Alvaro Domecq displays 'Spanish walk' at an indoor display at the Jerez school.

Photo:

Alvarez Domecq, whose name is given to the avenida, is one of those distinguished members of the family best known outside Spain for sherry production, but in fact equally involved with horse and cattle breeding.

The Domecq ranch produces some of the finest fighting bulls while also breeding pure bred Andalucian horses. The horses are used on the ranch as well as in the bullring and illustrate the almost symbolic relationship between horse and bull.

However, if we search for any one dominant personality who has influenced the revival of the Andalucian horse, it is difficult to ignore the claims of Alvarez's son, Alvaro Domecq Romero.

His father, Alvarez, was one of Spain's top 'rejoneadores' or mounted bullfighters. It is always difficult for anyone who has never witnessed a mounted bullfighter in action to appreciate the riding skills involved. It is also difficult for a rejoneador to earn the universal respect of the crowds, who are always very knowledgeable, and his colleagues, who themselves compete in the same arenas.

The highest honours have, however, been paid to Alvarez Domecq, for his contribution to bullfighting, bull breeding and also for his horsemanship. He also produced a son, Alvaro, who has made a truly gigantic contribution to the Andalucian horse.

Born in 1940, Alvaro grew up in the

environment of the horseworld. A talented rider from his earliest days, he soon decided he wished to follow in his father's footsteps and become a bullfighter. He then embarked on a glittering career and, when he gave his farewell 'corrida' a few years ago, parts of Spain seemed to come to a halt, some businesses closing to watch the televised performance.

His bullfighting career took him to the peak of the profession, but Alvaro Domecq had much more to offer.

All 'rejoneadores' have to train their horses to a high degree of skill in order to remain alive and therefore are nearly always possessors of high training abilities. The highest levels of horse training and riding do not always go together (thus many olympic dressage riders employ trainers) and to achieve both is as much as the most dedicated horseman can hope for. Domecq, however, became almost obsessive in his love for the Andalucian Pure Bred, wishing to raise the current standard of the breed as well as promote it internationally. Seeing the Andalucian's lack of stature in international dressage, he also wished to restore its old prestige.

Although brought up to breed and ride Andalucians, Domecq, in common with other riders, used cross-bred horses, incorporating Hispano Arab and English Thoroughbred blood to add endurance and speed to the agility common to the breed. He did not cease to use these combinations or have less appreciation of their qualities, but according to his own testimony, embarked on a love affair with the Pure Bred when riding a horse called 'Trianero'.

Seventeen years ago, in Jerez, Domecq was

The history of the Andalucian horse is intertwined with the Spanish cattle and the fighting bull. Many of the breeders are involved with breeding bulls aswell as horses.
This bull, having sired many successful 'Toros Bravos', has been given an honourable retirement at the home of the breeder, Don Jaime Guardiola. This charming picture catches the son of Snr. Guardiola in an affectionate moment which also conveys something of the deep sentiment felt by the Spanish horse breeding community towards their horses and their bulls.

Photo:

awarded the 'Caballo de Oro' trophy. He was embarked on a path which, although continuing to be deeply interested in bullfighting, Doma Vaquera and the traditional Spanish countryriding, was to increasingly involve itself in classical riding and the promotion of the breed itself.

He possessed great skills as a classical dressage trainer and rider and there is little doubt that he was an ideal candidate to head the revival in the breed's fortunes.

At the time Domecq received the Golden Horse trophy, he was at the peak of his bullfighting career. Almost a cult figure in his country, he was also a member of a family which had international links and great prestige abroad.

Appreciating the classical background of the Andalucian, Domecq perceived the need to both display its classical qualities and to promote public interest in the old classical school. Seen from a time before its inception, the scheme seemed beset with difficulty. To display the Andalucian in action before international audiences meant moving many horses, riders and equipment vast distances involving great expense and, even then, there was the problem of teams of riders capable of riding the classical movement and airs.

He decided to create a national school of riding and eventually this was established in Jerez. He gathered around him some of the finest riders and trainers in Spain, all imbued with the enthusiasm to successfully re-establish the breed's reputation. Antonio Moreno, Antonio Diosdado, Manuel Vidre and Luis Ramos Paul are names associated with the early days of the school. The list of distinguished and respected names is far too long to be mentioned here.

'Islero', runner-up overall in the stallion class at the 1989 Jerez Feria, is a fine example of the lighter-framed stallion. He is the property of Snr. Lopez de Vargas of Seville.

Photo: Judy Blake

The site chosen for the school was in the grounds of the old royal palace, itself only a short walk from the Avenida Domecq. Here a magnificent building to house the school was eventually built. Although a modern building, it has sufficient traditional style to blend perfectly with the palace itself. Since its formation, the school has trained many talented riders in the classical art and it is a mark of its success that professional teachers and trainers in Spain regard it as a cachet to be able to say they were pupils or riders of the school.

In addition to training horses and riders the school offers public displays of riding which show off the horses in classical quadrilles, airs off the ground and work between the pillars. These displays for the public are normally held once a week at approximately 11.30a.m. and the programme lasts for about an hour and a half.

The emphasis is on the grace and agility of the Pure Bred Andalucian and the phrase "Como Bailan Los Caballos Andaluces"—"how the Andalucian horses dance"—will be heard repeated over the loudspeaker introductions. And dance they seem to, accompanied by music that fits perfectly with their paces and programme.

The enormous finances involved in the project gave rise to many early problems. Now the school is under the Jerez town government and Domecq is its technical director. He is still often to be seen leading the riders in their performances.

The school takes a limited number of foreign students and offers a course of training in classic riding. It recently recieved royal patronage when King Juan Carlos presided over its inauguration as "The Royal

The author on 'Euclides', a stallion sired by 'Barbero' and bred by Snr. Joachin Rodriguez of Albacete.

Photo: Judy Blake

Andalucian School of Equestrian Art."

Over these early years, Domecq has dedicated his life both to the school and to the promotion and improvement of the breed. The school itself offers a perfect background for the public performances and these give the spectator a real glimpse of the Andalucian at work.

As you leave at the end of the performance, it is easier to see why the Andalucian horse dominated Europe for hundreds of years.

Those fortunate enough to have seen both the Jerez School and the Spanish Riding School in Vienna will certainly notice differences in style. They will see that the Jerez performances are perhaps not so mechanically perfect as those in Vienna, the Andalucians in Jerez appearing slightly more carefree, almost dashing in movement, compared to the metronomic gait of the Lippizaner in Vienna. This is not necessarily a criticism, since the national temperaments are not quite the same and the two schools are not sharing identical goals.

It is also necessary to bear in mind that the school in Jerez is still young and cannot have the formalized traditions of Vienna.

The Lippizaner, the closest blood descendant of the Andalucian, has nevertheless evolved into a breed destinct from, although close to, its ancestor.

Andalucian blood is still used to introduce new vigour into the old Lippizaner bloodlines and anyone fortunate enough to have ridden true examples of the two breeds will recognise their great similarity.

Will Domecq succeed in his dream of Andalucian re-entry into world popularity? Perhaps total success may be too much to expect and certainly he has suffered setbacks

This stallion breaks into 'Spanish Walk' quite spontaneously while being led to the show ring at the Jerez Feria. The natural high shoulder motion of the Andalucian enables it to learn this movement quite easily.

Photo: Judy Blake

206
JCB
OFIREX

outside his control. The current outbreak of African horse fever has been a severe blow. It has led to the closure of borders and the drying up of exports of Spanish horses. Many horse brokers and other businessmen associated with the horse's export have seen their painstakingly built up ventures disappear almost overnight. These individuals' move into other fields will leave a gap hard to fill when the situation resolves itself. However, that may be some time away.

Whether Domecq achieves his dream may be questionable but no-one can deny his enormous contribution to the Andalucian. His total commitment and his ability to bridge the gulf between countryriding and classical dressage, his breeding programme and his success in publicising the Andalucian make him one of the gigantic figures of the horseworld.

The magnificent heads of the three lead horses of a team of seven matching greys exhibiting in Jerez, 1989.

Photo: Judy Blake

The decorations on the bridles and harnesses of the teams of horses shown 'enganches', in carriage displays are handmade by traditional craftsmen. Each piece is assembled with great care and an owner who orders a new set may have to wait for several months before delivery. Each owner has his own colours.
The bridles are usually stored in cool temperature-controlled cabinets to avoid damage by insects.

Photo: Judy Blake

5

Where Now?

The question is often asked—"What of the future for the Andalucian?"

Given its undoubted qualities, it is difficult for anyone closely associated with it to be too pessimistic. We must not, however, underestimate the problems. As we have seen, the supply of good examples of the breed to the outside world may be cut off for an indefinite period because of African horse fever. This is a disease that appears very suddenly on the Spanish mainland and is a feverish illness which is in most cases fatal. It seems to appear at intervals of many years and can lead to the destruction of whole breeding herds.

To the breeder of Andalucians it is viewed with the same alarm as foot and mouth disease carries for farmers.

The eradication of the fever is most difficult. Not least because there is no absolute agreement on its causes or the measures necessary for its removal. This is not made easier by the lack of a central body with sufficient funds and authority to impose a solution even if one were readily available.

It is thought that the disease is imported from Africa, hence its name. It has certainly existed on the African continent for many years and an expert from South Africa recently attended a conference in Spain to advise in the light of African experience.

The illness is held to be transmitted from one animal to another by mosquito, in much the same way as the tsetse fly carries Malaria. This, of course, makes eradication extremely difficult. The mosquito borne by strong winds may well reach the Southern Spanish coast from Morocco—only fourteen miles

On previous page:

This black and white study shows the riders of the 'Real Escuela Andeluce del Arte Ecuestre' in the traditional costume worn for public displays.

Photo:

A team makes a tight turn at speed. Within the confines of the arena attached to the Military stud showground in Jerez, this manoeuvre calls for great skill and experience from the driver of the team.

Photo: Judy Blake

separate them.

Certainly once on the mainland, it only has to infect one horse. From there the local mosquitoes, also subject to winds, can manage the rest.

Whether in fact it is the African Mosquito or transported Polo ponies, is at present an argued factor, but in any event, the recent outbreaks started in the South and this appears to be the usual trend. Horses may be infected but not show symptoms, merely carry the organisms in the blood and so have it transmitted to another more susceptible animal. Talking to Spanish officals and vets, I have found no common agreement as to whether a carrier holds the potential infection for only a short time or not and there is certainly disagreement over the real value of inoculation. Does inoculation remove or merely hide the problem? This argument becomes more heated because of the complications some horses develop on vaccination.

It is, of course, extremely difficult to restrict the movement of horses. Immediately after the last serious outbreak, all horse movement was banned and horses anyway restricted from crossing province boundaries. Nothing, however, seemed to be able to stop riders exercising their horses on private lands, or in many cases on bridle paths.

Polo strings were still to be seen at morning exercise and some riding trekking centres offered business, although on a more curtailed area.

It was also noticeable that each authoritative body was reluctant to take unpopular and expensive measures. In government terms the horse comes under defence, a reasonable enough circumstance

In cross-country carriage driving slight errors of judgement often end in spectacular accidents.

This team ended in the water, but happily neither horses nor men suffered any injury.

Photo: Jamie

when the Military is the controlling body for breeding.

It is impossible to escape the feeling that strong political motives hindered authoritarian action. The Olympics were due for Barcelona and the idea of large numbers of fatalities publically announced was almost certainly unacceptable.

The Breeders' Association had neither the funds nor the overall authority to act and anyway, their export programme was in jeopardy.

For many reasons the death rate figures available publicly were less than those claimed by those involved privately.

At the time of writing, the British Andalucian Society has been told of a two year period before horses will be able to be imported from Spain. This may be shortened, but another outbreak just before the due date would be a terrible setback.

The African horse sickness is therefore a major obstacle at present to the restoration of the breed to international pre-eminence.

Other problems lie ahead. There have been great strides made in establishing studs outside Spain. In America the breed has achieved great popularity as a riding horse and there are many breeders. It must be said, though, the local 'type' commences, after enough generations, to develop along separate lines. Subtle differences in height, build etc., start to appear. One can foresee an 'American Andalucian' evolving which is distinct from its ancestors.

There are studs established in European countries and horses are available for sale in Germany, France, Holland, all producing pure breds of good quality but how long will the northern climate and pastures continue

If the Andalucian horse has special distinguishing characteristics it is reliability and wonderful temperament. This stallion exhibits this as it allows the children to play in its stable without any fear of injury.
Many horse owners and livery yards feel that a male horse, unless gelded, is a potential problem in a yard where mares are also present. They are surprised to learn that the Andalucian stallion is unlikely to cause trouble when in mixed yards. Its natural gentleness and calmness nearly always prevail.

Photo:

to produce the breed unchanged.

These are questions I have found many devotees unwilling to address.

In England, the British Andalucian Horse Society has made some progress in their breed shows towards publicising the breed. There are now certainly a greater number of good horses in the United Kingdom than a few years ago. It has to be said that the increased demand for these horses has not always helped the cause. For a period, too many poor or second class examples found their way into England and the society has had to accommodate them. However, the hard work and enthusiasm of the society has begun to pay off and the annual inspection by the Spanish Breeders representatives to pass young entries for breeding purposes is invaluable.

Don Alvaro Domecq, on his famous horse 'Opus', preparing to place the banderilla during the 'rejoneo'.

Photo:

6

Conclusion

In producing this book, I hoped to encourage the British riding public to take an interest in the Andalucian Pure Bred horse. I was encouraged to have the temerity to do so after failing myself to find anything on booksellers shelves dealing with this particular breed.

I hope this very brief book will help to show what a truly noble animal this is. I myself came to the Andalucian late in life. For many years I rode part-thoroughbred, part-Irish horses because their paces were suited to dressage, which paid off in competition.

During the early seventies, I had the privilege of training under John Lassetter then operating in Porlock.

John Lassetter had himself trained at the Spanish Riding School in Vienna and on leaving there brought with him four trained Lippizaner stallions. These were available to pupils studying classical dressage and were my first introduction to the Lippizaner. Superb schoolmasters, they taught me much I could not have learned otherwise and I have ever since admired this wonderful breed.

It was not until 1984, holidaying in Spain, that I first rode an Andalucian. My wife had read of a riding school offering scenic rides for experienced riders. I was on holiday and enjoying a break from horses.

I had a clear vision of the sorry sort of animals she would find there and felt I spent too much of my life with well-trained dressage horses to want to trek off in the hills on some broken-down riding school hack.

She came back from her ride full of enthusiasm and told me the riding master was an ex-Jerez School rider and had a horse

The rejoneador, Don Fermin Bohosquez prepares to place the banderilla. The horse shows a typical bullfighting movement which classical dressage followers will identify with the older battle training movement, 'Levade'.
The horse rears up, attracting the attention of the bull, which will then charge. Once the bull starts his approach the rider may decide which line to take so as to meet the bull at an angle which enables him to plant the dart in the bull's shoulder.

Photo:

at the stables working at Grand Prix level. On hearing I was a dressage judge, he sent an invitation to ride his horse.

At the time I declined but out of politeness went to the riding school to see the horse and meet the trainer. That was my introduction to Ricardo Donoso, a man of immense courtesy and charm who became a friend.

Later that year, I returned, this time on holiday with John and Dale Lassetter Hearing of our coming, Snr. Donoso insisted on putting his horses at our disposal. He knew of John Lassetter and was looking forward to meeting him. As a result, we did ride his horses and it was a grey stallion called 'Taranto' who converted me to the Andalucian horse. I was instantly struck by his beauty and presence. Donoso thought I should take him off into the hills and I set off, together with Judy, with some nervousness following two other riders. They soon went off at a rather fast gallop and I was left on a strange stallion that felt as if it might explode, with Judy, unsure of our way, either out or back, and decisions to make!

Taranto was magnificent. He went at whatever pace I asked and climbed and descended mountain paths that I would never have asked my own horses to attempt. By the time, a few days later, we returned to the U.K., I was an addict.

I found my own horses less pleasurable and each time I visited Spain, I became more involved.

It was inevitable that I would buy a Spanish horse and when Donoso told me of one for sale near Seville, I flew back to Spain determined to acquire him.

We drove to Los Palacios, just outside Seville, to the establishment of Don Luis Ramos Paul, who was then the horse's

In Spain the horse comes into its own at the ferias and the Spanish take their ferias very seriously indeed. The whole family takes part, and this young man in his 'vaquero' costume will one day be a rider in the parade.

Photo: Judy Blake

trainer. There I met Cariolo III, who was to finish the job started by Taranto.

'Cariolo' was six years old, a grey stallion who had started his training with Mercedes Gonzales as a four year old. He then went to Ramos, who continued his classical training.

His lateral work was excellent, his flying changes improving and he had started piaffe. He was also the most comfortable ride I have ever had. I bought him and after a while brought him to my home in Guernsey.

I did take him back to Spain for a spell but then transported him to Guernsey again. He gave me more pleasure than any horse I have owned and his death in 1989 from cancer was a major family tragedy.

During the time I had him, I sold my other horses because I found less and less pleasure in schooling them when 'Cariolo' was available. When he died I was devastated, but as is the way of life, I acquired another grey stallion during the year and I had already bought a young colt, presently in training.

Used to people saying stallions were too much of a handful, it is hard to accept that Andalucian stallions have such a superb temperament that most of them can be stabled in a 'mixed' yard and cause no problems.

They are very amenable to discipline and training. Their natural gait makes tham a superb ride, very comfortable in all paces. The newcomer to them must wonder why he spent so many years doing 'rising trot'. Eye-catching with great 'presence', they are a great boost for their rider's ego and I have never met a disappointed owner.

Anyone wishing to learn more of this breed should contact the British Andalucian Horse Society, or take an opportunity to visit one of the shows which include a class for the breed.

Members of the Spanish Breeders' Association

AGRICOLA CINCO LOMAS
D.J. Antonio Garcia Lomas y
Allen Perkins
Rosario Pino. 8
28020-MADRID. 91 279 97 03

AGRICOLA VALVI, S.A.
Avda. Villas de Cuba. Jardin 29
Bloque 6. 4°. Izda.
41007—SEVILLA. 954/52 51 00-52 51 21

AGUILAR GARCIA, D. Antonio
Colón 5
41440—LORA DEL RIO
(Sevilla). 954/80 09 90

ALARCON DE LA LASTRA DOMINGUEZ
D. Joaquin y Hnos.
Patio de Banderas. 16.
41004-SEVILLA. 954/22 57 02

ALBA AYALA, D. Francisco J.
Plaza de Cuba. 9-4
41011—SEVILLA. 954/27 19 94

ALBA ROMEU, D. Antonio
Carretera Cubellas. 2-27
08800-VILLANUEVA Y GELTRU
(Barcelona). 93/815 50 00

ALBERT ORTIZ, D. Francisco J.
Explotacion Agricola Ganadera
Lusane. 6-8°. A
08022-BARCELONA. 93/212 31 98

ALONSO GALLEGO, D. Juan Carlos
Pedro Perez Fernandez. 12
41011-SEVILLA. 954/45 14 51

ALORA, S.A.
Gerente D Luis Alonso Polo
C Aranda de Duero. 5
09002-BURGOS, 947/26 08 69

ANDRADA VANDERWILDE Y BARRAUTE, D. Francisco.
Plaza Siete Revueltas. 4
41620—MARCHENA.
(Sevilla) 954/ 84 37 36

AMANTE MADRID, D. Manuel
C. Gran Avenida. 34
03600-ELDA (Alicante). 96/538 18 53

ASENSIO ALONSO, D. Francisco
Moron. 18
41600—ARAHAL (Sevilla) 954/84 02 75

BALLESTEROS MORCILLO, D. Jesus
Heroes de T dedo. 43
14800—PRIEGO DE CORDOBA
(Cordoba). 957/54 01 43

BECERRA YERGA, D. Fidel
YEGUADA EL BARROCAL
Bulerias. 13
41410—CARMONA (Sevilla). 954/14 01 09

BERTOLIN BLASCO, D. Manuel
Doctor Moliner. 13
46010-VALENCIA. 96/369 79 93

BOHORQUEZ ESCRIBANO, D. Fermin
Plaza Angustias. 10.
11402—JEREZ DE LA FRONTERA
(Càdiz). 956/34 72 50

BOHORQUEZ RUIZ, D. Miguel
Alamos, 4. Monte Alto.
11401—JEREZ DE LA FRONTERA
(Càdiz). 956/30 78 93

BORT CANET, D. Vicente
Aptado. 87.
12580-BENICARLO
(Castellon). 964/47 12 00

BRAVO MARTINEZ, D. Ignacio
Finca "La Morera"
06370-BURGUILLOS DEL CERRO
(Badajoz). 924/54 12 78

BUIGUES OLTRA, D. Vicente
San Antonio. 26. 03700-DENIA
(Alicante). 96/578 12 44 - 578 54 75

CABALLOS ESPANOLES, S.A.
Tinte. 12. 02001-ALBACETE.
967/22 91 13

CAMACHO BENITEZ, Hnos.
Martin Belda. 2. 14940-CABRA
(Cordoba). 957/52 00 51

CAMARA YSERN. D.ª Rocio de la
Avd. Republica Argentina. 16.
41011-SEVILLA. 954/27 23 59

CARDENAS OSUNA, D. Miguel Angel de
YEGUADA CARDENAS
Avda. de Italia. 3. 41400-ECIJA
(Sevilla). 954/83 05 02

CARDENAS OSUNA, D. Pedro de
YEGUADA PEDRO DE CARDENAS
Ancha. 4. 41400-ECIJA
(Sevilla) 954/83 01 33

CASANUEVA CAMINS, D. Manuel
Marbella. 50. 28034-MADRID.
91/734 01 74

CASCANTE ALBA, D. Diego
Terno Galvan. 8.
41730-LAS CABEZAS DE SAN JUAN
(Sevilla). 954/86 90 86

CASTELLA DEL CASTILLO, D. Jamie
Finca Santa Alicia
41710-UTRERA (Sevilla). 954/86 14 73

COCA GARCIA, D. Ignacio
Finca "La Cepilla"
28690-BRUNETE
(Madrid). 91/811 01 50 (108)

CONESA CONESA, D. Joaquin
C. ª de Guadalupe s/n
Apdo. Correosn ° 28
06400-DON BENITO (Badajoz).
924/80 09 54

CORTES DE LA ESCALERA
D. ª M.ª Dolores
República Argentina. 16
41011-SEVILLA. 954/27 00 49

CORTES GARCIA, D. Salvador
Pl. Generalisimo. 12.
29640-FUENGIROLA (Málaga)
952/47 43 95

CORTES RODRIGUEZ, D. Antonio
General Sanjurjo. 4.
18600-MOTRIL (Granada)
958/60 07 38

DEHESA "LA GRANJA"
Gavilanes. 6. 28035-MADRID
91/419 15 97

DIAZ NAVARRO, D. Juan
Cortijo Ardón. 23760-ARJONA Jaen
953/52 31 84

DIOSDADO PALACIOS, Hros.
de D. Antonio
Sto. Domingo. 11
11405-JEREZ DE LA FRONTERA (Cadiz)
956/34 10 26- 17 19 52

DOMECQ ROMERO, D. Alvaro
Recreo "El Paquete"
JEREZ DE LA FRONTERA
(Cadiz) 956/31 47 47

DOMECQ ZURITA D.ª Blanca
Apdo. 310
11480-JEREZ DE LA FRONTERA
(Cadiz) 91/650 03 52

EL ESPARRAGAL, S.A.
Conde de Ybarra. 23
41004-SEVILLA 954/22 45 47

ERQUICIA GUARDIOLA, D. Alfredo
Cortijo "Jedulilla"
11630-ARCOS DE LA FRONTERA
(Cadiz) 956/70 08 51

ESCALERA DE LA ESCALERA
D. José Luis
General Armero. 83.
41420-FUENTES DE ANDALUCIA
(Sevilla). 954/83 71 65

ESCALERA DE LA ESCALERA
D.ªM.ªFernanda
Habitat 7. nº 1-2º 6
41007-SEVILLA
954/51 47 39 — 83 73 22

ESPINOSA DE LOS MONTEROS,
D. Eugenio
Alberto Alcocer. 13
28016-MADRID 91/250 87 52

EXPLOTACIONES AGROPECUARIAS, S.A.
D. Miguel Arpa Battle
General Mendoza. 1
17002-GERONA 972/20 05 77

EXPLOTACIONES AGROPECUARIAS
"CASTILLA, S.A." "AGROCASA"
Apartado de Correosn 17
05080-AVILA 918/21 10 77

FERNANDEZ-DAZA y FDEZ.
DE CORDOVA, D. Francisco
Reina Victoria. 13
06200-ALMENDRALEJO (Badajoz)
924/66 08 68

FERNANDEZ FERNANDEZ, D. José M.ª
FINCA EL ARREBOLADO
41710-UTRERA
(Sevilla). 954/86 02 25

FERNANDEZ MONTES, D. Joaquin
y D. José.
San Felipe. 15
41410-CARMONA (Sevilla).
954/14 08 70

FERNANDEZ ORDAS, D. Aniceto
Paseo Pintor Rosales. 18
28008-MADRID. 91/247 50 01

FERNANDEZ DE LA VEGA Y SEDANO,
D. José Maria
Plaza del Caudillo s/n
45870-LILLO (Toledo). 925/17 01 00

FERNANDO A. DE TERRY, S.A.
Santisima Trinidad. s/n
11500-PUERTO DE SANTA MARIA
(Cádiz). 956/86 27 00

FERRERO FIOL, D. Fausto
Joan Miro. 255
07015-PALMA DE MALLORCA
971/72 70 36

FOLGAROLAS GENERO, D. Ramon
Jaime I. 5. 6.º 2ª 08500-VIC
(Barcelona). 93/886 18 62

FOMENTO AGROGANADERO
MANCHEGO, S.A. FOGOMAN, S.A.
Director Técnico: D. Alfonso Segura Nájera
Ctra. Camon s/n.
Apdo. Correos 187
13005-CIUDAD REAL 926/22 04 20

FOMENTO GANADERO EXTREMENO,
S.A. FOGEXSA
Avda. República Argentina. 22-bis-3º A
41011-SEVILLA. 954/27 08 88 - 27 09 83

FRAILE GARCIA, D. Aquilino
San Francisco Javier. 13 -4 ºA
41005-SEVILLA 954/66 36 48

GANADERIA LAS LUMBRERAS
Director Técnico: F. Jacobo Delgado
Sol. 27. 41760-EL CORONIL (Sevilla)
954/87 72 46

GARCIA DIEGUEZ LOPEZ, D. Miguel
Julio César. 4 - 1.ºB
41001-SEVILLA. 954/21 25 54

GIL MARIN, D. Jesús y D. Miguel
Goya. 47
28001-MADRID. 91/275 98 05

GOMEZ CUETARA FERNANDEZ
D. Juan
José Rivero. s/n
28590-VILLAREJO DE SALVANES
(Madrid). 91/874 40 00

GOMEZ RUBIO, D. Galo
Pozo. 18
13500-PUERTOLLANO (Ciudad Real)
926/42 07 84

GONZALEZ DEL VALLE, D. José M.ª
Marqués de la Vegade Anzo
Paseo de la Castellana, 126
28046-MADRID. 91/261 24 47

GRANDA LOSADA, D. Miguel
Conde de Campos de Orellana
10291-ALDEA DE TRUJILLO (Cáceres)
927/32 03 67

GUARDIOLA FANTONI, Hros. de
D. Salvador
Plaza Calvo Sotelo. 5
41001-SEVILLA. 954/22 67 16

HACIENDA "LA PLATA"
Conde de Ybarra. 4
41004-SEVILLA. 954/22 40 37

HAMMOUDA BOUZIDI, D. Mohamed
Avda. Eduardo Dato. 22 -Bajo
41005-SEVILLA. 954/22 50 53 - 86 80 01

HARO GUZMAN, D. Enrique
C/. Horacio Lengo.n.º 12.6º-1
29006-MALAGA. 952/32 79 12

HEARST, D.ª Joanne
Virgen de la Antigua. 30
41011-SEVILLA. 954/27 78 11

HERVELLA GARCIA, D. Jesus
Avda. Jose Antonio. 29
34002-PALENCIA. 988/72 08 35

JARAQUEMADA OVANDO, Hnos.
Hros. Marqués de Lorenzana
Corredera. 35
06360-FUENTE DEL MAESTRE
(Badajoz). 954/27 05 87

JIMENEZ MONTEQUI, D. Ignacio
Reina Victoria, 18. apartado 4.
03100-JIJONA (Alicante). 965/61 01 92

LASTRA RAMOS PAUL
D. ª Concepción
Pedro de Valdivia, 19 bis - 28006-Madrid
91/262 01 46//954/22 50 53

LAZO DIAZ, D. Francisco
Hacienda Lerena
41830-HUEVAR (Sevilla). 954/75 60 61

LONGO ALVAREZ DE SOTOMAYOR, D. Pedro
Avda. de Eduardo Dato. 47
41005-SEVILLA. 954/57 12 74

LOPEZ GIBAJA, D. Antonio
Libertad 20
28100-ALCOBENDAS (Madrid)
91/652 18 14

LOPEZ MARTIN, D. Francisco
Avda. República Argentina. 20-5.°
41011-SEVILLA. 954/27 27 72

LOPEZ MENDEZ, D. Rafael
Sta. Catalina. 2
21200-ARACENA (Huelva).
954/27 60 61

LOVERA PORRAS, D. Enrique
Jesús Maria, 16 - 1. °Izqda.
14003-CORDOBA. 957/23 92 86

MARQUES DE SALVATIERRA Y HNOS.
Apartado de Correos 59
41300-SAN JOSE DE LA RINCONADA
(Sevilla). 954/38 13 00

MARIN GARCIA, D. José Luis
Palos. 7-5. °
21003-HUELVA. 955/24 09 18

MARTIN IGLESIAS, D. José A.
Pertinez Quesada. 19
18140- LA ZUBIA (Granada).
958/59 00 80

MARTIN LORCA, D. José Luis
Hotel Angela. Paseo Maritimo
29640-FUENGIROLA (Málaga)
952/47 52 00

MARTINEZ BOLOIX, D. Mannel
Avda. Blas Infante. 22
14730-POSADAS (Cordoba).
957/63 08 95

MARTINEZ LORA, S.A.
D. José Luis Martinez Orti
Capitán. 12 29640-FUENGIROLA
(Málaga). 952/47 09 14-46 13 71

MAZA INIGUEZ, D. Pedro
Amadeo Deprit, 4
48006-BILBAO
94/412 70 12

MESDAG, D.ª Klaas
Hacienda "La Gamera"
29140-CHURRIANA (Málaga).
952/43 50 80

MIGUEL-ROMERO GOMEZ-RODULFO, D. Antonio de
Marqués de Borja
Diaz Calvo. 2
06700-VILLANUEVA DE LA SERENA
(Badajoz). 924/84 20 39

MIURA FERNANDEZ, D. Eduardo
Isaac Peral. 5
41012-SEVILLA 954/61 42 46

MONTANO GALAN, D. Francisco
Asunción. 63-5°A
41011-SEVILLA. 954/45 00 24

MONTIJANO CARBONELL, D. Carlos
Avda. República Argentina. 32
14004-CORDOBA. 975/23 51 68

MORENO DE LA COVA, D. Alonso
Monasterio de San Francisco
14700-PALMA DEL RIO. (Córdoba)
957/64 31 92

MORENO GARCIA, D. Jaime
Yeguada Los Arcos
Mesena, 45
28033-MADRID. 91/202 78 50

MORENO GARCIA, D. Manuel
Juan Pérez Zúniga, 24
28027-MADRID. 91/267 18 07

OLIVERA BERMUDEZ, D. Francisco
Cortijo "Olivera." Apdo. 181
41580-ALCALA DE GUADAIRA (Sevlla).
954/70 13 15

PANADERO LOZANO, D. Andrés
Escritor Mercado Solis, 7
14011-CORDOBA. 975/27 18 47

PAZ JIMENEZ, D. Francisco de la
Hacienda San Agustin
Ctra. Mairena del Alcor, Km. 9
41510-MAIRENA DEL ALCOR (Sevilla)

PEREZ TABERNERO, D. Alipio
37450-MATILLA DE LOS CAÑOS
(Salamanca). 923/21 94 96

POL TORNERO, D.ª M.ª Luisa
Plaza 18 de Julio, 3
41002-SEVILLA. 954/22 84 63-22 12 53

PORTILLO GIJON, D. Eduardo
Plaza del Punto, 1-2. °-D
21003-HUELVA. 955/24 96 98

RAMIREZ DELGADO, D. Ismael
Alfonso XIII, 17
VILLARALTO (Córdoba)
975/11 73 95

RODRIGUEZ SEVILLANO, D. Luis
Avda. Castilla, 7
28280-EL ESCORIAL (Madrid)
91/890 13 02

ROJAS PALATIN, D. José M.ª
Avda. de la Borbolla, 51
41013-SEVILLA. 954/23 32 88

RUMASA, S.A
Velázquez. 50
28001-MADRID 91/435 69 25

RUIZ SANCHEZ IBARGUEN, Hnos.
Asunción. 30
41011-SEVILLA. 954/27 32 87

SAGERAS Y ALCAZAREN, S.A.
Plaza del Conde. 4
37500-CIUDAD RODRIGO
(Salamanca). 91/234 40 69

SAN MIGUEL USLE, D. Manuel.
Can Morató
08440-CARDEDEU-LLINAS
(Barcelona). 93/846 09 04

SANCHEZ BARBUDO MARTIN, D. Salvador
Avda. de la Borbolla. 51
41013-SEVILLA. 954/23 37 85-6

SANCHEZ BEDOYA Y FERNANDEZ MENSAQUE, D. Antonio
Reina Mercedes. 33
41012-SEVILLA. 954/61 05 10

SANTANA CARMONA, D. Fernando
Luz Arriero, 6
41010-SEVILLA. 954/33 50 62

SANTOS REDONDO, D. Mariano
P. ° Carrascal. 13
(Segovia). 911/10 71 34

SENORIO DE BARIAIN, S.A.
Ctra. de Alange, Km. 8. Apdo. 310
06880-MERIDA (Badajoz). 924/31 46 63

SENORIO DE SIRRA BRAVA
D. Joaquin González Barba
Avda. Victoria. 34
41012-SEVILLA. 954/37 37 00

SES ROTES, S.A.
Marqués de la Cenia, 39
07014-PALMA DE MALLORCA
971/22 66 42

TRIQUELL CALVET, D. Francisco
Jacinto Verdaguer. 3
08205-SABADELL (Barcelona).
93/725 61 33

TORRE PARRAS, D. Vicente de la
Avda. de Espana, 29
02002-ALBACETE. 967/22 28 53

URQUIJO Y NOVALES, D. Juan Manuel de
Conde de Odiel
Aptado. 9
41720—LOS PALACIOS Y VILLAFRANCA
(Sevilla). 954/86 50 38

VALENZUELA, Hnos.
República Argentina. 2
23700-LINARES (Jaén). 953/69 48 09

VARA MUNOZ-CASILLAS, Hnos.
Plaza de Espana. 20
06100-OLIVENZA
(Badajoz). 924/49 01 52

YEGUADA ALCANICES
Duque de Alburquerque
Castello, 98-3 °
28006-MADRID. 91/629 00 01

YEGUADA JOSE M. ARISTRAIN DE LA CRUZ
Finca Valdepuercas
10137-ALIA (Cáceres)

YEGUADA CANDAU
Cerrajeria, 12.
41004-SEVILLA. 954/22 33 03

YEGUADA CATALA
D. F. Pablo Catalá Garrido
P. Pais Valenciano. 4
03760-ONDARA (Alicante)
965/76 61 24 - 76 68 33

YEGUADA LOS CIERVOS
D. Antiono de Lorenzo
Avda. Valladolid. 81
28008-MADRID. 91/247 02 24

YEGUADA FRANCISCO SANTIAGO RUIZ
Marquesa, 4
29005-MALAGA
957/21 85 91 - 21 85 58

YEGUADA HATABO
Virgen de Luján. 22
41011-SEVILLA. 954/27 29 58

YEGUADA JAPON
D. Antonio Pérez Japón
Avda. Villas de Cuba. 13
41007-SEVILLA. 954/52 17 75

YEGUADA MAIPE
Plaza de los Tres Reyes. 1
30201-CARTAGENA (Murcia).
968/50 84 50

YEGUADA MANUEL DE LA CALLE
Avda. del Carrascal. 17
11407-JEREZ DE LA FRONTERA (Cádiz)
956/30 75 10

YEGUADA PLAZA DE ARMA
D. Florencio Moreno Munoz
San Juan Bosco, 18
14400-POZOBLANCO
(Córdoba). 975/10 05 43

YEGUADA PESQUERIL
D. Antonio Esturillo Peragalo
D. Nicasio Guillen Garcia
Blas Infante. 2
41440- LORA DEL RIO (Sevilla)
954/80 04 69-80 17 36

YEGUADA HNOS. RODRIGUEZ MARANON
Virgen de la Antigua. 7-1 A
41011-SEVILLA. 954/45 31 40

YEGUADA ROMERO BENITEZ
C. NARANJAS. 4
11404-JEREZ DE LA FRONTERA (Càdiz)
956/35 05 51

YEGUADA LA TRINIDAD
Hnos. Rojas Maestre
Reyes Católicos. 6
41004-SEVILLA. 954/21 13 73

YEGUADA LA TROYETA
Mesón Troya. Ctra. Las Rotas.
03700-DENIA
(Alicante). 96/578 14 31 -578 55 64

YEGUADA VALDEZARZA
Hnos. Fernández López
Alcalde José M. ªde las Heras 2
28530-MORATA DE TAJUNA (Madrid)
91/873 01 06

YEGUADA VILAIRE
D. Samuel Vilaire Cifre
Capitán Gual. 50
Fax. 971/54 76 38
07400-ALCUDIA
(Baleares). 971/51 50 57

ZOIDO MONTORO, D. Benito
Generalisimo. 28
23300-VILLACARRILLO (Jaén).
953/44 00 74

Index